An Exodus of Sparks

An Exodus of Sparks

POEMS BY **ALLISA CHERRY**

Wheelbarrow Books ▪ *East Lansing, Michigan*

Wheelbarrow Books
Michigan State University Press
East Lansing, Michigan 48823-5245

LIBRARY OF CONGRESS CATALOGING-IN-PUBLICATION DATA
Names: Cherry, Allisa, author.
Title: An exodus of sparks : poems / by Allisa Cherry.
Other titles: Wheelbarrow Books poetry series.
Description: East Lansing, Michigan : Wheelbarrow Books, [2025] |
Series: Wheelbarrow books poetry series
Identifiers: LCCN 2024021005 | ISBN 978-1-61186-521-9 (paperback) |
ISBN 978-1-60917-775-1 | ISBN 978-1-62895-539-2
Subjects: LCGFT: Poetry.
Classification: LCC PS3603.H483 E96 2025 | DDC 811/.6—dc23/eng/20240520
LC record available at https://lccn.loc.gov/2024021005

Cover design by Erin Kirk

Visit Michigan State University Press at *www.msupress.org*

With the publication of Allisa Cherry's *Exodus of Sparks*, the Residential College in the Arts and Humanities (RCAH) Center for Poetry at Michigan State University offers its fourteenth book in our Wheelbarrow Books Poetry Series. Clearly, we pay homage to William Carlos Williams and his iconic poem, "The Red Wheelbarrow." Readers will remember the poem begins "so much depends upon" that red wheelbarrow. In our country today, with significant issues of climate change, inflation, covid variants, cultural fracture, and political unrest, many people would say their lives do not depend upon poetry. Far from it. Ezra Pound told us that "Poetry is news that stays news." This is not "fake news," or yesterday's news, or old news. Good poems have immediacy, present us with specific people in specific situations, not unlike our own, and, most of all, poems tell us the truth. "The first function of poetry is to tell the truth," June Jordan reminds us, "to learn how to do that, to find out what you really feel and what you really think."

In a 1988 essay, "Four Temperaments and the Forms of Poetry" (*American Poetry Review*, Sept./Oct., pp. 33–36), Gregory Orr proposed that there are four distinct temperaments that poets can be born with, and the strongest poems are those that exhibit in some form all of those temperaments—story, structure, music, and imagination. While Orr is focusing on and discussing individual poems, I would argue that these four temperaments combine not only in individual poems but also in the strongest and most powerful collections of poems. This is certainly true in *An Exodus of Sparks*. Allisa Cherry tells us stories of family, stories of trauma and tragedy in that family, stories of personal experience seen through the lens of Biblical characters and apocalyptic experience. The collection includes a crown of sonnets focused on the body of Moses, poems in couplets, poems long, and poems spare, the structure of each poem determined by its content.

And there is music throughout the poems: "He is the canyon / I carry inside me. / A cranium full of relentless light," lines that occur in the very first poem. A bit later, we encounter, "And outside her window where the wind / moved through the eucalyptus / that baked all day in the valley heat / and scented the yard with honey." Near the end of the collection we find "Heron, teach me how to tell my blind mother / the way you lift above nettle and ash in flight." Alliteration, assonance, consonance, and cadence all make music through the lines. Finally, imagination, the ability to connect disparate elements, to make metaphor, to surprise us with juxtaposition. "There is a depth in every desert / where you might as well be / in the middle of the ocean, the stars / tattooing an SOS across a silence / that spreads out for decades." And one more: "Years ago / I dropped a whole religion. It fell / from my grasp and splintered / to matchsticks on the basement floor."

In *An Exodus of Sparks*, we encounter a narrator who remembers the deaths of her brother before he was twenty; her father, glowing with the radiation he was exposed to by being a downwinder, someone exposed to radioactive contamination from nuclear testing in the desert Southwest; and her mother, succumbing to blindness before her death. "Because of the way I / cannot keep myself / from looking back," readers are given the stories of the narrator's struggle with and within her family, with her religious beliefs and upbringing, with America, who "flexed your nuclear / muscles in our direction 1,054 times / over the length of my father's short life." Memory, mystery, missing persons from our lives—they're all here. The collection opens with this line, "I am a stranger here."

Allisa Cherry understands we are all strangers in so many aspects of our lives. We try to make sense of our relationships, events that impact our lives, histories that inform our own. In the final poem, "An Exodus of Sparks," as the narrator imagines her father's return from the dead, she says "our raised voices throw sparks, / threaten to burn down this wilderness of grief." Earlier, she has given us the image of blue "sparks / cascading off the anvil," an iron block on which metal can be hammered and shaped. Allisa Cherry hammers out her grief about so many things on the anvil of these poems, her words, the sparks that that can ignite the wilderness of our own grief, our own losses. Her father, she tells us, told her, "*Everything / you have you must share / with strangers.*" She has done just that in these poems.

As our number of Wheelbarrow Books increases, we hope that our audience increases also. Help us spread the word. In the beginning was the word, we're told, and the word became the poem. So much depends upon the collaboration of reader, writer, and poem, the intimate ways we come to know one another.

—Anita Skeen

An Exodus of Sparks centers on a people, not as an abstract landmass, but as lives and the loss on which they have been built. They pass through these poems, die, resurrect, share cruelty, and partition love. They inhabit a world where new growth is quickly crushed beneath a bootheel. The collection remains attentive to shimmer while delivering an unflinching indictment of an existence where "the praise of labor / is always answered with more labor." It is an undeniable force, a book of disillusionment with inherited faith, and a homage to constitutive grief.

These poems leave a physical record in the reader, as when in "Without Any Warning," a scene of intrafamilial violence unfolds into a "compression of love and history / in those landed blows." Their figurative play is cutting, almost unmerciful. In "Revelations," an Avon lipstick sample is "the size of a bullet casing." In "The 13th Article of Faith," a bishop admonishingly asks for a reflection, and a language unfolds into "nouns that might be used / by a cosmetics company / for different shades of lip gloss," leading up to the bishop's imaginative unveiling as a rancher with "one desire," "to drive us / like cattle toward God." The book itself is a dilatory unveiling. Poems, such as "Redemption Is Too Quiet," "Here I Take," and "Slip," lead us through the revelation that "there is no gospel / on the Colorado Plateau / No mansion. / No holy ghost building. / It is somber / where we gather."

Poverty acts as a structuring force, taking the shape of a sermon, an intimate scene, and a dissection table. It structures what each person expects of life and is embedded in their joy, as when a young cheerleader in "Southeast of the Nevada Proving Ground" stands "with other teenagers / waiting for a nuclear blast on the horizon." In "Valley of Dry Bones," the speaker's father paints "a series of abstracts," struggling "to make something / beautiful rise up / from this irradiated wasteland / even as it split him / like an atom," making us question the role of the artist. Here is a man trying to paint his own destruction, someone's father.

As the poems progress, they become more and more speculative. In the section titled "Daughter of Downwinders," a man's wife commands him to live, and "he obeys / because he fears her / more than he fears God." The body of

Moses comes to life in a harrowing series, and the screen door between the living and the dead is held open, beckoning us to come inside. This baring of language eventually helps the speaker shape another role, moving from the assigned familial roles into a new family, where she must consider the extent to which the memories that she carries in her flesh will shape who she becomes.

While reading *An Exodus of Sparks*, I felt myself drawn into a wholly unfamiliar world, one I will never become part of, and yet I came to feel as if these were my brothers, mothers, and neighbors. It struck me that this was what the best poetry does. Rather than speak to strangers in their language, it guides us through its own. It does not cater to an imagined other nor assume a common understanding. It creates a parallel space populated by ghosts and the lives they haunt, so they may converse or argue on equal footing.

—Roque Raquel Salas Rivera

for Ivan, Dianne,
Kevin, Kristen,
Matthew, Bethany,
and Jason

Contents

An Exodus of Sparks

Salt River

I am a stranger here.
I strike out and disappear
into the echo of my name,

follow it down a craggy seam
where juniper and cedar brush
jut into a blue as white as an eggshell.

I abandon the rock
where I carved the date
of my father's birth.

*

My father is dead
and can only visit me
in silence. He is the canyon

I carry inside me.
A cranium full of relentless light
that tells a borrowed story.

But the voice that repeats it
is my own.

*

How will I praise him
in this desolate land?
Where will I go
now that I've dusted my shoes
of the irradiated soil that took him?

North toward the rim
past settler housing gutted
by winterfat and gumweed

plucking wildflowers
before they have the chance
to bloom until the day
I am allowed to rise

from the shadows of the canyon floor
to a terrible brightness
that knows my given name.

I.

But your carcasses shall drop in this wilderness.

—*Numbers 14:32*

Unreadable

Sometimes I misremember and I
am the one looking out the clinic window
when the SUV speeds through a red light
and hits the drunk as he sprints into the street
flinging him up and over like he is
made only of his soaked clothing.
But the truth is my back was turned.
Or how else could I have seen
the lightning strike of terror
cross my daughter's face and moved
as if the wet sound of body upon asphalt
were her own head splitting open.
Why else did I lunge toward
the tender warmth and hum of her
before I followed the other woman
who dropped her purse on the white tile
and ran outside to part traffic around
the young man's body—her hand thrust out
like Moses before the Red Sea.
It was pouring rain. I knelt at his side
and made him a tent with my coat.
Blood from a cleft in his temple
eddied in an oily puddle. I pushed my fingers
into the soft folds of his throat seeking a pulse
and felt a terrible lonesomeness flutter
beneath my own skin. I asked him
his name—I know I did—though the sound of it
slipped into a current of shock
and was carried away. In the distance
a train blew its whistle and farther still,
the moan of a siren moving too slowly toward us.
When I was young girl in Sunday school

I imagined the multitude of fish
suspended in those massive cliffs of seawater
must have been so perplexed watching
the Israelites walk across the ocean floor
as they hung there, a wall of unblinking eyes,
their round mouths opening and closing.
The world seems to be a certain thing
until a moment illuminates the text
so brightly it becomes unreadable.
When the medics arrived, I left the man
and returned to the building where my daughter
watched me from the other side of the window.
My daughter, who I send into this violent life
over and over. And I held up my bloody hands
to show her I could not open the door myself.
Looked into her eyes—blown wide with fear
and wonder—and asked her to let me back in.

Without Any Warning

I think of my father's black eyes
blood vessels broken

and the sick olive green of his skin
turning sallow

in the days that followed the fight
on the basement stairs

where a bare bulb lit
my brother's ascent

his fists flying, his mouth
spitting sparks as he rose.

How many nights before my father
paced a rut through time

watching for my brother's headlights
to swing into the driveway.

How my brother once let me sleep
against his rib cage

the night the planets all lined up
and I thought

we were going to die.
Without any warning

the compression of love and history
in those landed blows

the old man's joints slowing
as he pulled

his punches and allowed my brother
to rise and win

while my brother's friends watched
from his bedroom door.

The blown glass bong upended.
The Crown Royale sack

of D&D dice dropped and scattered
like bright jewels

across the unfinished floor.
And the next morning

how they proceeded to love one another again
sheepishly at first

with swollen jaws and bruised knuckles.
How a light poured

through a fist sized hole in the drywall
and illuminated our mother

as she told us we must tell the neighbors
my father fell

carrying the baby on his shoulders.
That his hands reached up

and instinctively protected
the baby when he fell.

Revelations

Naked from the waist up and still
wearing her Sunday shoes,
my grandmother sits dead center
at the foot of her bed.

Lacewings and plume moths
batter the bulb on the back porch.
My brother reads a *Mad Magazine*
down the hall. I came

when she called me. I stood
perfectly still and watched
as she unbuttoned her blouse
to reveal two livid scars

where her breasts had been.
Now the shock of that battered skin
pulled taut across her rib cage
is like staring at a blighted field.

So I focus on the vanity mirror
behind her where I can see
the tender expanse of her back
and my blank face rising

like a moon over her shoulder
until the shiver in my locked knees
recalls her to her nakedness.
She pushes her fists into her

shirt-sleeves, buttons up her blouse.
And because I do not cry
she lets me pick two Avon
lipstick samples from a sandwich bag

she keeps in her garment drawer.
Each is the size of a bullet casing.
I choose a pink the color of trout meat
and a red, more ruby than blood.

Still, Small Voice

The June bug she finds tangled
in a knot at her scalp
has sticky legs and a carapace
so thick she can hear
her fingernail click against it.

When she reaches up to scratch
the tickle in her hair and startles
her praying family with a scream

does her father think
the Holy Ghost moves through her?

The Holy Ghost does not move through her.
All those late nights she only hummed
"*Give* Said the Little Stream"
because she was afraid of the dark.

Give away, oh give away she whispered
until she convinced herself she might
become invisible through service.

And outside her window where the wind
moved through the eucalyptus
that baked all day in the valley heat
and scented the yard with honey

and pine, she decided the Holy Ghost
could live there. Not within her, but near.
And between them, a curtain she could draw.

Now her father marches her
from the family room,
untangles the beetle from her hair
and laughs until the corners of his eyes

seem etched with Hebrew *shin*
as he gazes with wonder upon the June bug

pinched between his thumb and finger,
its barbed legs rotating
mechanically in the air.

The 13th Article of Faith

The bishop said *think on these things*
but we didn't know if he meant chastity
or virtue, benevolence or faith.
All nouns that might be used
by a cosmetics company
for different shades of lip gloss.
We thought *imagine*
only ever kissing one mouth
for the rest of your life. He said

Follow the admonition of Paul
and we heard Bono singing "40"
The Edge's voice entering
high in the octave.
We wanted each subsequent year
to be a new mouth
opening toward us
filled with longing and praise.

The unfashionable tie
knotted at the bishop's throat
made us think of a tether.
How he'd lashed himself to his woman
like a raft on a swollen river.
His eyes did not brighten
before the shine on our mouths.
He was steadfast. He belonged
in the company of ranchers.
He had one desire.
He meant to drive us
like cattle toward God.

Family Violence in Five Acts

i.

You find me climbing the dying elm
to watch cottonwood seed cluster
and blow across the grass. You throw
a lit brick of Black Cats at me.
I nearly fall to my death.

ii.

You say *make my lunch*
and drag me to the pantry.
I punch your neck. You've torn
my skirt to the waistband.
You mama's boy!
You stick-figure!
Tucked in the country
among rough jocks and hicks

you are slowly becoming
the thing you hate.

iii.

I clear Grover's Hill barefoot
before you run me down
in the pickup truck. You drop me
like rolled sod over the tailgate,
drive me home down Main Street,

iv.

throw me in the yard
and turn the hose on me.
The cold water tastes like copper.
So does the split in my lip.

Hair dripping down my neck and back,
shirt bunched and sticking across my chest,

I cry *Truce! Please, truce!*

You agree to stop
if I promise not to tell.

v.

Before I get to the screen door
you slam it and bolt it between us.

Forehead pressed against the mesh,
thumbs in your ears, you goad me.

I grab a monkey wrench from the tool bench
and swing it against your skull.

After the *crack* and just before you fall

my victory settles like dust between us.
And I know I love you, brother,

staring at me, wide-eyed
like you are seeing me for the first time.

Redemption Is Too Quiet

There is no gospel
on the Colorado Plateau.
No mansion.
No holy ghost building.
It is somber
where we gather.
We whisper
sister / brother
when we pass
below the hum
of the air conditioner.
The silver
sacrament tray
is cold. The bread
white and full of sugar.
Each thimble-size cup
shivers with the miracle
of transubstantiated
tap water. But at home
my father's hard heels
tap on the parquet tiles
when Harry Belafonte
plays on the stereo.
And each time she hears
"Boulder to Birmingham"
I know my mother
imagines a full choir
singing it over her grave.
In the basement
my brother mimics
Jimmy Page
and Tony Iommi

on his electric guitar
all the way down
to the roots of his hair
standing on end
and waving
like an acre of grain
before harvest.

Rolling over Fitfully

Brilliant heavenly body
shooting through
the night sky
    —stars
        —ground
    —halo
        —moon
    —sweat
—glass
    —dust
restlessly spinning
toward a quilted
landscape like
a sycamore seed
to rest upon
red clay
    (broken crown)
yellow stone.

Here I Take

The road's black quiet selvedge.
The yellow cheatgrass
grown right to its shoulder.

How it bends softly toward center.
How it pulls me to the internal line.
I drive fast. Cedar brush

blurs into unbroken hedgerows
I cannot see beyond.

I second guess myself. I forget
then remember the cliff you went over.

It was early in September—still hot.
Still filled with the sting of deer flies.

And you in your concert T-shirt
and your mismatched socks
were not dressed for death.
You were dressed as though

you were ready to enter
the beginning of everything

You were not dressed
for the brutal work
of razing our father's house
when you took to the task.

You salted his gardens
and tore out his paths.
Now isn't our God

a belligerent god. He never
enters when called upon.
He creates exits in unholy places,

the shoulder of a little-used highway,
a hospital shower, the parking lot of a bar.

Here, he took my surfeit of sunshine.
The steep incline lined with velvet scrub
seems almost kind.

It should have passed you gently
hand over hand and set you down softly
never to rouse from your drunken slumber

never to wonder at the crack in the bend
where forever two things might happen.
Like a rough-legged hawk

you rise up and dive over.
Or you wake up just in time
and lean like the cheatgrass
back toward the centerline.

Slip

A woman struggles
to pull her dog's dead body
off the freeway slip road.

She is as old as my mother,
wears a sheer cotton house coat.
I can see the outline of her thin legs
in the sunshine.

*

Every Sunday my mother stands me
in the picture window
to check for light bleeding through fabric

so she might spare the congregation
the silhouette of my young thighs.

*

My mother says her mother
wore the same tattered slip for years
so she could afford new ones
for her daughters.

*

The dead dog is heavy, its head
the size of an Easter ham. The woman
leans into her burden, slips,

takes small steps to regain her footing,
face set to her task. The morning air
sweetened by magnolia blooms
is slow. Those crude chores

done dead center to our deepest grief
are awkward and absurd
but they stitch a mourner to time.

*

My mother says put on a slip
before we leave for my brother's funeral.

Madonna of the Trail

> They were just as brave or braver than their men because, in many cases, they went with sad hearts and trembling bodies. They went, however, and endured every hardship that befalls a pioneer. —*Harry S. Truman, at the dedication of the first Madonna of the Trail statue, July 2, 1928*

Free of her plinth and no longer
heavy with clinging children
her skirts billow, cast a shadow
across the parking lot of Western Drug.
She rises through pink and yellow dust,
begins to drift like fallout from Nevada
or neck feathers plucked from the last healthy hen.
She has the same broken heart as my mother.
They share a vocabulary.
They sing the same hymns.
And when she is gone

the velvet pile of night
absorbs the hand that once
stroked it. And one by one, the stars
fall into the Little Colorado.
Absence pushes its seed into faith,
all night promising this emptiness
will be the new frontier.

Mogollon Rim

Light falls at an angle
along the forested path
like knives sliding into a knife block.

And my father's swollen knuckles
threaded between my small fingers

puts an ache in my hand.
I spent a sleepless winter
watching the moon outside my window

grow fat and thin
while my father lamented
his dead son. Now I am,
you might say, afraid of him

as we set out like Isaac and Abraham,
our faces red with cold.

When we arrive where the pine grove
splinters into a clearing
a quiet descends
around a mule deer giving birth.

Her wide eyes fixed inward.
Her burnish undulating
over the motion of an unborn fawn.

A sprint coils in my haunches.
my tongue drops
from the soft palate of my mouth.

I want to rush
toward this swollen moment.

But my father
is already pulling me back
into the tree line
whispering *hush*.

The Cold That Settles Lifts

That poor cadaver
resting in the dissection lab
might be in her sixties.
But the skin over her ribs
peeled neatly back
looks like a young cormorant
ascending from a salt marsh.

In order to really see her face
haloed by lank hair shot with silver
eyelids as thin as onion skin
I have to drown out the brutal chatter
of other biology students
circling the table.
And when I palm her liver
passed to me like a sacrament tray
I find its weight

contains a waning glory.
We are young.
Some of us just beginning
to fall in love, our hopes pinioned
by that withered red knot
slick with glycerin. Some of us
think we're ready to see her dead body

but when the sheets are pulled clear
the backward hush of revelation
is like holding a nest of fledglings
in our mouths. So that years later

when I lay my hand
upon my father's still breast
fingers unfolding
across his burial whites
I will think I hear
the babble of many voices
or a murmuration of starlings
lifting in flight.

Bleached to Brightness

My father's terry-cloth bathrobe
had a long white sash and
hung from a hook in the master bath
where I wasn't allowed to go
after I got caught spying
on my naked mother
drying her body off after a shower.

But sometimes I snuck back there
to bury my face in it.
Nobody else in our household
owned such a fine garment.
It smelled of tobacco and bar soap,
oil of clove and table salt.
I rarely saw it on him. But once

when I returned from church
he was wrapped in it—clean
and sleeping. I stood over him
and loosened the knot,
pulled it open like a tent flap
or a temple veil and beheld
the scrim of silver hair over his belly,

his scrotum and penis on his pale leg.
All so soft it was as though I saw him
through layers of moving water.
And I began to understand
the tenderness of Joseph,
his hand upon his father's thigh,
promising to take his body
away from Egypt to be buried.

Southeast of the Nevada Proving Ground

Consider the young cheerleader
who stood beside a blue swimming pool
with other teenagers
waiting for a nuclear blast on the horizon
by which she timed her best
herkie jump into the air
while everyone applauded.
The radios spoke into the whorl
of each listening ear,
saying that America is most secure
as the sky unzipped itself
and a light more infinite
than its container
bloomed toward Las Vegas.
A hundred detonations in the atmosphere.
Eight hundred and twenty-eight below ground
where the cheerleader's cobalt bones
now radiate
beneath the sterile dirt
seventy years into their half-life.
Her toes are pointed.
Her arms make an X across her breast.
After all this time it appears
she is still rising
midway toward a leap
just before her body
leaves the earth
and arrives at air.

Valley of Dry Bones

Remember, our father
painted a series of abstracts
using only sanguine red
and a cream
the pale brightness
of a cow skull
bleached on the desert floor.
Remember, when he wasn't
writing code for a computer
that was as large as
our family room
and levitated above
its own thrum and hum,
he wove God's Eyes
from brightly dyed yarn
on crossed sticks
or planted eucalyptus
and built sandstone paths
for the tender succulents
he had to water by hand.
Remember, our father struggled
to make something
beautiful rise up
from this irradiated wasteland
even as it split him
like an atom.

Daughter of Downwinders

i.

Mind pitted by the fentanyl drip
dripping reprieve into his
burning body, my father
loses the thread of time
and mistakes me for a stranger
standing beside his hospital bed.
I tell him, *Remember*
I'm your daughter
and he demands that I prove it
by showing my back to him.
So I, obedient to the very end,
turn, unbutton my blouse and
tug it down till the small
worn stones of my upper spine
and the shadows between
my shoulder blades
are revealed to him.

But before all this, I once
brought my guitar to his room
so I could play for him.
Half-way through the first song
my throat opened like a gate
and a stone fell out. I thought
I heard a violent flutter of wings.
But it was only footsteps
rushing to the doorway
where three nurses appeared,
breathless. And one said
Oh, honey. We thought he
had died and you were crying.
And my father couldn't stop laughing.
My father found it delightful.

ii.

In Apache Junction,
my great-uncle
pulls his broken washer
from the wall and is stung
by a small bark scorpion.
His heart fails.
His wife finds him
dead in the mudroom
where a honeyed light
pours through the dusty window
over his old body.
She commands him to live
and he obeys
because he fears her
more than he fears God.
I'm starting to think
I can't die
he tells me from the only chair
beside my father's hospital bed.

And then a silence
opens between us.
And my father's body,
glowing with radiation,
falls like a star right through it.

iii.

In the undeveloped fields along Rio Salado
ocotillo buds dart from their stems
like embers escaping a fire. I drive
five miles an hour below the speed limit
under an evening sky darkening
in raw-seamed layers. Somewhere
deep in the bluffs I know
the clean sails of the sacred datura
are pinwheeling open.
Their spiny seedpods hidden
at the base of their stalks. Their blooms
the size of a newborn's head.
I used to believe if I could only master
the arcane art of being a daughter
it would be enough to fix my father.
But today I watched his vision
worry a small tear in the veil
beyond which he said he could see
his dead son's headlights
swinging back up our old driveway.

In the bluffs datura blooms.
And deep in his bed my father's face
brightens to see his son finally
returning to him. Like a detonation
in reverse. Or a flower closing.
Or a sky-blue pickup rolling
up the side of a cliff. Inside
my brother—beloved skull
intact—tuning the radio
drunk and laughing.

Fatherland

The dry grasses left
by the Herefords
rattle like bone slivers
in your red clay soil.
Cottonwood pods
cluster at the fence post.
A crow eyes the Coke bottle
between my knees.
I do not love you,
Arizona, and I said
I would never come home.
Now hours from the border
my sister's eyes
are two basins of water.
It is only a mirage
that I ripple toward her
like a highway
at its vanishing point.
Where a ship might
emerge from a seam
between this life and the other.
A ship captained
by our dead father
conveying his kin. All made
of silver compounds.
Overexposed and shimmering.
Inexplicable on your skyline.

Sage: A Note to Self

I regard the velvet bracts,
the blooms forming whorls
along woody stems and know
that a violent blue answer
levitates like mist
above an otherwise tawny stretch.
It clutches at my breath.
Before I use the word to praise a man
when everything he's grown

he's dried and crushed
beneath his bootheels,
I'll remember how a sage shrub
brushed by a horse's flank ignites
a hundred small pilot lights.
Sage from salvia/salvere/to save.

This is how I will arrive at salvation.
I'll pull Moses
from the deserts of Judea,
place him in Apache County.
I'll say he ran like a mustang
before God's children.
That he gathered them back
from the sage where they strayed.

II.

And the presence of God withdrew from Moses,
that his glory was not upon Moses;
and Moses was left unto himself.
And as he was left unto himself,
he fell unto the earth.

—Joseph Smith, Pearl of Great Price, Moses 1:9

The Assumption of the Body of Moses

Once it was enough to picture the boy version of you
pulling wings off winged things. Sufficient to pack
the spaces rooted out with yarrow and honey
and know that you were always un-adorable—a terror
I didn't know how to care for. Truncated and squalling
in the estuary. Startling snowy egrets into a blizzard of flight.
Even the smallest version of you, tongue twisting like a yucca root
inside your mouth, could not ignite the fires of my compassion.

My dear, the end is never contingent upon
a single thing. My hands exhume your body
from Moab's shadowy folds. In those yellow
and suede hills that hold you, I weave a crown
to claim my own authority. From your knucklebones.
From tamarisk sprigs. From acacia spikes.

The Mortification of the Body of Moses

A crown requires a hawthorn spray, ripe with
healthy blood-red haws. Each persistent calyx
affixed by God who lies as naked as a newborn
in Cedar Mountain's shadowy lap. He attaches them
one by one. And when he is done he whispers vowels
into the hindmost of your breastbone. His gold-capped
teeth gild the tips of my name with phosphorus.
Matchsticks and tinder lie in the salt flats of your mouth.

My love, in order to speak it
you must first breathe it
past the flint and friction in your throat.
Flames will scar your lips shut
around embers. I will live out my days,
a cinder upon your tongue.

The Corruption of the Body of Moses

Cinder to tongue, my mouth pulls you
beyond the ululations of foreign courts.
Like a skittery deer upon Mount Tabor
I dance to make you look at me. I would even
pay the scribing fee if our wedding could be
an endless ceremony that never arrives
at marriage. You return, sullen, shining. My
bridegroom-bride, you are promised to another.

And still, I want it to be you
who sews the apron to my nakedness.
I would just as soon trade my lyre, love,
this book and all its vocabulary,
my robes, my rings and my sandals,
for your mother's temple veil.

The Radiance of the Body of Moses

I would rather be a shredded temple veil,
a wobbling circle drawn in the dirt, rent sackcloth,
or a pile of ash on your liver-spotted crown than live
as the stutter in your mouth. Even the static electricity
in a robe's dry folds would be warmer than this
woeful harangue. Have you forgotten? You once ran
like a mustang before God's children and brought
each one back through the sage when they strayed.

Let us go from here, darling, before we
shame ourselves. See? The seraphim
gored by your radiant face turn
their molting backs to you. Ophanim
blow feathers around the throne dais
as sullied and light as prayer.

The Appropriation of the Body of Moses

The longer I carry you the lighter you grow,
a posy of feather, bone and salt,
borne over the ocean by an emigrant bride to a home
that is not your home. From the terebinths of Abraham
to the paloverde stretching from La Coyotada
to the Coyote Mountains, where my Elders ran
from Pancho Villa's army along with their
many wives. Can it matter anymore that I stole you,

Bone-of-My-Bones? I hold you. Splinter
in my throat. Shard in my eye. Fracture
in the chambers of my heart. There are no clouds
over the tabernacle of this desert. When the setting sun
strikes the flint of the canyon rim the sparks
ignite us. And we go up in flames like a bush.

The Interment of the Body of Moses

The final ember escapes from the bramble
but the bramble remains, burnt and twisted
on the canyon's rim. And the moon rises,
centered in its ashy branches, pale,
whittled, anemic. The ghost of my heart in my
rib cage, drumming *let go, let go, let go.*

Sweet faith, I don't know who I am without you.
Unrecognizable, without land or family.
I pack my lungs full of juniper and lie down
beside your tired bones, your untied tongue,
in a warm and quiet arroyo where water
will never again run. Never disturb the quail's
clutch in the shelter of your thigh bone. Never
trouble the jackrabbit asleep at your breast.

III.

Then God spake to Moses' soul:
"My daughter, one hundred and twenty years
had I decreed that thou shouldst dwell
in this righteous man's body, but hesitate not
now to leave it, for thy time is run."

—*The Legends of the Jews*

Depth of Field

Moving from a dark house
to a bright yard
the aperture narrows

In the chicken run
a single ink cap pushes
through damp straw

Low storms gather
beneath the unfolded wings
of ducks rushing the yard

The heart, too, dilates
as the body brushes against
what has remained wild

Each galvanized second
unbearable in that it
cannot be borne away

That light does
dance around the umbo
of a mushroom cap

That the eye says only
this flower, this daughter,
this footpath, this star.

Moses, When Sleep Descends

It is a thousand crepe-winged
sycamore seeds. I dream of you,
if by *dream* I mean no longer
hem in thought's tattered fabric
where you trail, Loose Thread,
worrying the back of my leg.
If by *you* I mean your absence.
Everywhere I look, you are
not. Every door to sleep opens
into rooms where you do not bide.
And your absence is not
the rough brush of winter bedding
against collarbone and throat
nor the thoughtless press of pubic bone
to mattress ticking. Your absence
is a thorough lonesomeness. I crave
to be Borremose Woman, pressed and saved
below a thousand pounds of heather and sedge.
My ears stoppered, mouth stilled, eyes
darkened to the threshold of you
departing. To be both light and flightless
is to be forever
suspended in a stillness
of which you are not part.

Bless the Damage

Now that time has nacred over
the rough edges of memory
I can say that you were a real beauty.
A shiner. You glittered like glass shards
in the baby formula. I mapped my way
forward in the darkness
by the pulsing gleam of you. Sometimes
the lung-stopping quartz in the quarry
and sometimes the toothy drill—
its circumference as wide as two bodies
entwined, bearing down and fruitful.
When I finally got to Oahu I was
no longer with you. I sliced my foot open
on a bit of coral. It was my first time
snorkeling. The first time I'd seen
a school of fish. My presence small
before a wall of countless eyes,
I felt—for the first time—beheld.
Back at the hotel, I sat on the sink
and scrubbed the wound out
with bar soap and a toothbrush,
feeling resourceful but alone.
And it wasn't the sheen casting off
the warm water or the ribbon of blood
unwinding that I found most compelling,
but how the cut resembled a lightning strike
across the arch of my foot—plumped up
with white blood cells rushing to the infection.
How the tight red skin looked like it might
burst into bloom the way the peony buds
you sent to my new apartment bloomed.
They were still petal-dense knots

when they arrived. And I got to watch
the entire life and death of them.
The almost obscene way they swelled open
and then the velvet bowl of each petal
falling empty across my kitchen counter.

Cuckoldry

Viewing porn in which a wife
clutches her husband's face
and makes him watch
as she gives her neighbor a hand job,
I am aroused
not by the confusing stretch
of entire pink nakedness,
the actors throbbing
in a knot like plucked foul.
Nor by the three veils of voyeurism.
Instead, it is the quality of pretend shame
shifting across the husband's face
like mist skirting
a shallow body of water

that moves me.
How he forgets
and then remembers to emote
when his wife calls him weak,
when she says, *you like that, don't you.*
This world can be hard on a cuckold.
Maybe he gets through these moments
the way I survived my marriage:
creating grocery lists,
checking my phone messages,
browsing nature clips on the internet
where I once found a video of a cuckoo
hatching among another bird's clutch
and was stirred
not by the abandoned bird
nor the way it struggled as soon as it emerged
hopelessly fragile and pink
to twist and writhe and shove

the other eggs from the nest
before they hatched.
Sometimes, in my human heart
I resent how nature conspires to feed itself.
But as the cuckoo bulged
beyond the constraints of the bower
a perfect yellow ring
grew around her eye
encircling both mote and beam.
And her song grew lovelier, too.
Each trill became a hollow reed
for another trill to push through.

To God, the Guidance

Being married to a drunk is like being a compass
in bed with scattered magnets. My intellect
honed to a brightness smaller than a penlight.
Smaller than fishing line or sewing thread.
As small, in fact, as the utmost atom
in a needle's point spinning recklessly
on its jeweled pivot. I am
a well-made, nonfunctioning thing.
Land doesn't exist. Instead
let me arrive at a moment
beyond all other moments.
Let my vessel be a time machine.
Return me to my mouth.
My language confounded,
the *liahona* in my apron pocket
waiting for a message from God
who only ever whispers
East. Southeast. And *South.*

Rattle the casing. My compass,
a box of angry bees. God,
its violent thrum. Pray
the fondant plug is not consumed
until the hive softens to its new queen.
That life doesn't end in a honeyless collapse.
That a young wife doesn't wander the waters
with a wooden box full of dead bees.

Hospitality

I bob like a float
in the Great Salt Lake
unsinkable

where the gulls that once
saved my people's crops
from a cloud of grasshoppers

rise and drop
for brine shrimp

shattering the thin crust
that lies over the shallows.

*

My father lived
by the laws of hospitality.

He told me *if the only thing*
your host has to feed you
is a bowl of blood soup

you will eat until the bowl
is empty. He said *everything*
you have you must share
with strangers.

If you sat beneath
the shadow of his roof
he would salt your food
from his own salt shaker.

*

Because I am my father's daughter
I opened my door to you

—red-faced, hang-dogged
your Peterbilt cap in hand—

and I offered what I had:
fresh sheets
in the spare bedroom,
water from the tap,
tomatoes so ready
they split open on the vine.

But what you took was
None of those things, baby.
And later *None of that.*

*

What do I mean
when I say *I am*
my father's daughter?

A thing
as necessary
and inexpensive
as table salt.

*

I never want to rise
from this body of water

to feel my weight
return to me.

Each salinated abrasion
received through these
guest/host transactions

sings a battle hymn
Onward! Onward!

while my heart hardens
like a starched brocade

because of the way you received
without mind or mercy.

Because of the way I
cannot keep myself
from looking back.

Miriam Alone Is Punished

> And the cloud departed from off the tabernacle; and behold, Miriam became leprous, white as snow: and Aaron looked upon Miriam, and behold, she was leprous. —*Numbers 12:10*

Raisin cakes, apples,
brown honey dripping
off a chalky comb.

The sky parts
and drops speech
into her mouth.

Electricity, breast milk,
cantaloupe, loam.
Perhaps by *Cushite*

she means *dark and lovely*.
Maybe by *married*
she means *yet gone*.

No matter. She speaks
against flesh and blood,
bewildered.

Though God once
talked through her
and she abandoned nothing,

the skin drops off her.
Bone broth, shortbread,
chicken fat, foam.

The Vessel and the Emanation

I buried the last duck beneath the red cedar
where the raccoon caught her
spading her slender bill in the dark soil.

She had wandered for two days
confused by a sudden lonesomeness
after her last companion died from a neck wound.

The infection so rapid
she'd unfurled her black wings once
and could not fold them up.

When the nesting crows called to the last duck
she would call back to them.
Each sound sought its sister sound
and returned to her

hollow and hungry.
If I made a list of all the things I cannot save

it would begin with you and me,
the ducks, and the garlic harvest,

money, time, my breath,
which escaped my body
like a damask ribbon when I found her—
meat torn from her breast

spine visible
and as milky
as a strand of baby teeth.

Her delicate head, a tendril of smoke
tangled in the morning glory.

Entropy Grips the Garden

Send me out into my ruin
where every twig shoots like a pistol
and every branch cuts like a sword.

Free me from chores and let me
maraud the undergrowth
in a swimsuit the color of hard candy.

Sweet and deadly, let the morning glory
strangle the grape arbor
and the ants overrun the clusters.

There was a time I thought I could
pull enough weeds to earn my keep here,
lay enough sandstone or scrub enough floor.

But the praise of labor
is always answered with more labor.
This life doesn't quit

shoving green growth down my throat.
The fruit trees, bearded with lichen
and bees, deafen me. The pansies

muscle past paving stones
and wreck the paths.
With each minute I tarry

I can hear my father
tabulating what I have cost him.
The space I occupy is borrowed

and will soon close over me.
Left too long,
the bittercress goes to seed.

Stigmata

When I gave birth,
my mother
was there. Her distance,
too, was there.
Her ice-cold
permanent love, there.
A monolith of quiet.
The room agitated around me.
Every hot atom
ricocheted close
to my singular purpose.
But not my mother's atoms,
a perfection of stillness.
When she pinched my right palm
with her bloodless thumb
and index finger, she made
a cylinder of chill
that drove through me
like a nail and left a wound
I could push a life through.

The Original Hyperlink Was the Word

and the Word was a door that a brother
and sister would walk through together
and end up in different rooms.
They could hold each other's hands—threaded
fingers locked at the knuckles—step over
the Word's threshold and find themselves apart.
I say the word *door* and you stand
before a framed variant of light.
You say *door* and I find my forehead
pressed against particleboard
inside my first bedroom in Arizona
before our father installed the knobs.
Eye to the bored-out hole, I can see
your eye staring back at me. I say *eye*
and you sight down the barrel of a rifle
at an empty field from a hunting blind.
You find no limit to the stillness there.
You say *eye* and I touch the crepe-like skin
of our mother's face. I can feel where her joy
multiplies but not her long aversion to sin.
I say *sin* but I mean *weakness*.
You hear *weakness* and you are standing
in your briefs on cold tile while other boys
bustle and sweat around you.
You aren't sure which part of your body
you should cross your arms over. I hear *body*
and I disconnect like a phone from its cradle.
I tell you *cradle* and you see me for the first time
decades and decades ago—squalling and pink.
The hall light shines through the crib slats
and leaves bars made of darkness
across my sleeping form. You say

the word *darkness* and I have arrived
at your house before sunrise,
newly divorced and unbundling
my four-year-old out of her car seat.
She is round in her winter clothing.
Milky-warm with sleep.
I bury my face in her fur-lined hood
until the buckle unfastens with a *click*.
But the Word doesn't wake her.
She hardly even stirs.

Forensic Ornithology

My daughter has bundled up many deaths
in old dishrags and brought them to my kitchen
—chickens torn by raccoon claws,
baby robins gutted by crows in the street,
small featherless scrub jays
nudged from their nests—
to peer like a haruspex
into their broken bodies for the trapdoors
where their souls dropped out.
Once, after a two-year absence, I watched her
inspect her estranged father the same way.
When he arrived, she was precise in her affection.
She was exact in her sorrow when he left.
My longing on her behalf is full of salt.
I could wring it out and make an estuary
where sandpipers and egrets gorge on small gray fish.
If I were to tell the truth here
I would say I resent how vulnerable I am to her
measurements and her calculations. Before her
I, too, could determine how much to love
and when. Now I round out my days
watching her leave through the doorway
with her breakable bones and delicate membranes,
worry caged like a house finch in my throat.

Ghost Ship on the Desert Floor

For the longest time I couldn't drive
with my feet in shoes, couldn't trust the shift
unless the grit of the clutch pedal
abraded my toes. I thought I had to work
for everything. I once raced Monica
all the way to Concho Valley.
We cut six minutes
off the twenty-minute drive.
Her Honda was faster than my pickup
but she was afraid to push the engine.
We sped down that adolescent median
that divides wanting not to die
from wanting to be alive
while my parents played spades
in my grandfather's double-wide trailer
moored out there to the shadows
of the Concho Country Club.

There is a depth in every desert
where you might as well be
in the middle of the ocean, the stars
tattooing an SOS across a silence
that spreads out for decades.
Barnacles multiplied
over the slow shutter of my heart valves.
My hands clung like starfish
in the dashboard's amber glow.
And beneath the Blue Clay hills
the fossilized bones
of megafauna
swam like whales.

Exegesis

It is because of my brother,
who will never be twenty,
I comb the land around Lyman Lake
seeking in its rough folds
that fracture where he gave this life
the slip. As if it might be marked
by a Utah juniper, its trunk
slowly twisting in a high desert wind,
its dusty blue berries
a door code I will punch
and finally enter a room
where it is always the moment
before his head splits upon stone.
Where the stars keep spinning
toward daybreak and the pickup
still teeters at the end of its long roll.
But it is hidden from me

by a nimbus of sage,
by threadleaf groundsel
popping off its yellow sass,
and snakeweed hiding the sinister truth
that he was not made to outlast me.
Someday soon, the lupine will rise
like blue spears from the dust.
The globemallow will bloom
to be devoured by ants.
And I will see his death
happened everywhere at once
so the earth raised a thousand descansos
that said *here* and *here* and *here*.

Let a Double Portion of Your Spirit Be Upon Me

Just before I left that town for good   you and I stood
in the front yard   knock-kneed   while I crimped your forelock

with a curling iron   and led you   untacked
to Main Street   for your last Pioneer Day Parade.

Placid   broken by years of labor   you let me
press my eye   so near to yours   all I could see

was a resolute darkness.   In that moment
I thought we might worship   the same god.

Which is to say   I felt we were both   shying away
from the dilation at the center   of an undefined spook.

Everything you were   saddled with:
every cruel rider   kicking calf   every thrown shoe.

And even me   the computer programmer's daughter
who once wanted to prove   she could drive

fifty head of cattle   across the *mal país*
and slapped the reins   across your withers.

I hoped one day   you could forget it all   and become
only speed   and the bend in the landscape   froth and flank

a shiver between   the short and long pastern   the matte
of your elegant bones   finally resting   cleansed by sunlight.

A Life / Mislaid

It began with the smallest things.
Earring backs and tubes of lipstick.
Estradiol structures. Dropped
stitches on salvaged dresses.

Growing over time to all
the books I hadn't finished
reading and all the annotations
I'd made in their margins.

Well-worn shirts I liked
to sleep in. All misplaced
in places I've since forgotten.
I watch the sun drop

behind a row of houses
and wonder how little I worry
about its absence. I enter my room
and a nameless cat stretches

toward a square of light on the bed.
My mother, this year, lost to me.
Being a daughter, gone.
Not like a twig snapping

or a radio switched off,
but an idea as thin as fog
burning off a warming lawn.
My own daughter, I've lost her too.

Summer became fall eighteen times
and she slipped over the bridge
in her silver hatchback. Years ago
I dropped a whole religion. It fell

from my grasp and splintered
to matchsticks on the basement floor.
Now I carry the bundle
and strike each one by one

to shine a path through the darkness.
The universe is not where I left it.
I can no longer find it without retracing
all those pinpricks left by the stars.

The Eros of Small Details

The pearl bead, the sand
in the corner of an eye,
the saliva
turning to powder
like milk on a baby's mouth.
The good sleep.

Once, when I was a young girl
I woke from a broken fever
and was afraid
someone had come in the night
to stitch my eyelashes shut.
I called out
and my mother came
with a wet rag.
She laid it across my face
until the sleep softened
and I could open my eyes again.

What warmth,
what desired assistance is sewn
into every affection since then.
And, too, what fear.
And also, what blindness

But this did not begin as a poem
about the way my mother loved me.
It began with you, asleep beside me,
naked and strange.
Ragged skin around your nailbeds.
A shadow bundled
to the hollow of your throat.

Unsighted

Heron, teach me how to tell my blind mother
the way you lift above nettle and ash in flight.

Your lanky grace pulls
into a density of bird. You become

a lowercase *m*, extend a swim stroke,
then push the earth downward

while you remain a fixed point
this world, this river, this boat we are on

spins around. She could still see a little
when my daughter first appeared,

eyes smeared with delta silt and mine
filled with her. Both landmass and water,

my mother and daughter
had just enough time to peer at each other

through that bright blur of emergency love
before her world went completely dark.

When the river guide says a bald eagle
can make out a rabbit's eye

a mile away, I hold my mother's hand.
You tilt and your wingtip dips into the river

like a blade. No. Like the starched lace hem
of a wedding dress. I ask her if she remembers

how cold Christopher Creek felt
in the springtime. None of her children

could wait for summer and we slipped in,
pain and joy, two hands squeezing

our hearts to death, our bones aching,
advancing into cold white

breathless laughter. Heron,
by the time I tell her that rapture

is what you look like breaking into flight,
you are so far down river you've become

the braille symbol for zero, a null banking
toward the backwaters before you disappear.

Your Spirit Might Rise Up and Go Before You

the way a doe
lifts her head

when she hears
the action of a rifle.

Put another way
you are the bed of the river
but you are not its rushing water

nor are you the doe
that browses its banks,
that hears a cartridge
slide into the chamber

and startles toward the sound
before it runs away.

*

God speaks
to Moses's spirit
while Moses is distracted
by his approaching death.

Moses's spirit tells God
she loves this body
and does not wish to leave it.

God calls his spirit "daughter"
and the tenderness of it hammers
on the anvil of your heart.

*

Tonight, your teacher plods
far into the midrash
to crack you open.

But it does not mean
he loves you.

Nor does it mean
he doesn't love you.

The only thing you can know
is the thread in the tzitzit
of his tallit is blue

not like the echo
that follows the pounding.
But blue like the exodus of sparks
cascading off the anvil.

An Exodus of Sparks

i.

America, you flexed your nuclear
muscles in our direction 1,054 times
over the length of my father's short life.
1,054 catastrophic blooms
shattering the desert floor,
confounding the waters and the heavens.
It took us years—decades even—
to realize the full arc of our swoon
before you, America. You buckled
your own soldiers down in the trenches
repeatedly. They prayed before you
and you revealed their hand bones
glowing beneath their skin. Pigs squealed
in aluminum barrels all around ground zero.
Ranchers wept before discolored cattle.
You strolled onto playgrounds waving your
Geiger counters over children frightened
by the arrhythmic crackles and clicks.
America, your mouth was one round
radio speaker repeating over and over
that you would never harm us as you
stroked your two-headed lamb and
straddled your babies. My father
was so small when you began to powder
his milk teeth and bones with your radiation.
It drifted across the Southwest as quiet as pollen
while his body swung through time like a net
gathering up your shining particulates
until one day his DNA lit up
in a conflagration of letters. America,
the last time you flexed your nuclear muscles
in our direction, my father was almost dead

from cancer. You called your final test
Divider and never once looked back.
Still, he believed in you
until his last monitored breath.
America—face resplendent, amber eyes
blazing—my father's ruination. When he died
his curled hand looked like it still
clutched at your garment's bright hem.

ii.

As my mother's heart begins to fail
my brother starts hearing voices.
He argues with the void,
screams at empty space
Get out of my room!
In February my sister films two episodes.
In the first, my brother
thumbs through a magazine,
his posture a tight C around it.
The room is full of sunlight.
His glasses are on the floor.
He slaps his hands around his ears
as if he's troubled by a swarm of bees.
In the second, my brother jabs
repeatedly at a dark corner,
his eye sockets an angry white. He takes
an aggressive drink from a Coke bottle
as if it were a beer and it spills
down the front of his shirt. I can hear
my sister's measured breaths off-camera.
She is the daughter
that never forsakes my mother
nor abandons my mother's son.
Still, I wish for freedom for her.
That she would remove her dress
slip from her temple garments
and let them spill like quicksilver
between her fingers. That she would climb
into cement shoes and fall forward
into the fathoms. And then
I hope I never see her again.
That she stays down there

until the second coming.
Light shattered and falling softly around her.
Ears deafened to our brother
playing a funeral march on his own skull.

iii.

When my father returns, his hair
will be as soft and white as thistle seed.
And everywhere he goes, he'll
shuffle his feet like an old man
in the only shoes that still fit him.
One hand will drag an oxygen tank
as small as a travel bag behind him.
The other will grip a long tube
connected to a port in his belly.
As I clamber toward my father's house
I realize I no longer love this drive
through the Salt River Canyon's
horseshoe turns and death-drops.
The way its walls hide a car wreck
in every hatcheted fold. The way
shadows pool beneath its dusty scrub.
How the road shivers like a congregant
moved by the spirit. Or how my siblings
are always there waiting for me
on the other side to watch my faith unbraid
into rivulets with less and less water.
But I must come this way to pick a fight
with my sisters and my brothers, to scrap
with them until our raised voices throw sparks,
threaten to burn down this wilderness of grief.
Because this is how we'll summon the ghost
of my father who wants to remain in this life.
And he'll appear in a doorway, his new hair
transparent against his gray-green skin,
the only part of him undiminished—the quantum
of light in his eyes. And he'll ask us w*hat are you*
fighting about? desperate to be himself again.

And we'll say *nothing that matters.*
And *would you like a glass of water?*
And *here, let us help you back to bed.*

NOTES

Still, Small Voice. In 1 Kings 19:12, in the King James Version of the Old Testament, God speaks to Elijah in a "still, small voice," following his victory over the prophets of Baal. Mormons often use this term interchangeably with the term *Holy Ghost.*

The 13th Article of Faith. Written by Joseph Smith in 1842, "The 13 Articles of Faith" are thirteen statements that explain the basic doctrines of The Church of Jesus Christ of Latter-day Saints.

Madonna of the Trail. The Daughters of the American Revolution commissioned twelve *Madonna of the Trail* statues to be placed in towns along the National Old Trails Road, including Springerville, Arizona. Dedicated on September 29, 1928, the monument was moved once in 1958 to accommodate the town's first traffic light, and again in 1987 to its current placement, wedged between a McDonald's and a shopping center parking lot.

Bleached to Brightness references Genesis 49:29.

Southeast of the Nevada Proving Ground. The Nevada Proving Ground was established in 1951 and was the site of 928 nuclear tests over the next four decades.

Daughter of Downwinders. The term *downwinders* is used to describe people who were exposed to radioactive contamination and nuclear fallout due to extensive nuclear testing as well as people and communities who were exposed to ionizing radiation due to the production of nuclear weapons, nuclear energy, and nuclear waste. Because of a remarkable increase in various cancers and other health issues among these populations, Congress passed the Radiation Exposure Compensation Act in 1990, often referred to as the Downwinder's Act. Several years after it passed, my mother was "awarded" $50,000 for my father's death by esophageal cancer.

The Appropriation of the Body of Moses. Many Mormon polygamists fled to Chihuahua, Mexico, and established colonies in order to escape persecution and prosecution from the United States government. In 1912, they were driven out of the territory by Pancho Villa's revolutionary forces.

Moses, When Sleep Descends. The preserved body of the Borremose Woman was discovered in Denmark in a peat bog in 1948. Carbon dating puts her at 2,790 years old, give or take.

To God, the Guidance. In Mormon tradition, the object called the *Liahona* is believed to be an ancient compass used by the Mormon patriarch Lehi, father of Nephi, to lead his family from Jerusalem to the American continent. Latter-day Saint scholar Hugh Nibley put forth the theory that the word is related to a "queen bee" or, alternately, that it translates as "to God is the guidance." There is no linguistic evidence to support these claims.

Miriam Alone Is Punished. See Rashi's commentary on Numbers 12:10.

The Original Hyperlink Was the Word. This title is pulled from something poet Eduardo Corral once said during a craft talk.

Exegesis. A *descanso* is a small monument built at the site of a violent, unexpected death, quite often the scene of a car accident.

Let a Double Portion of Your Spirit Be Upon Me. This title is taken from 2 Kings 2:9 (Amplified Bible) and was a request by Elisha to the prophet Elijah before his death.

Your Spirit Might Rise Up and Go Before You. Moses's final days are described in great detail in *Legends of the Jews*, 3:7. On his last day, after Moses has pled his case to remain in this life, God addresses Moses's spirit directly, using the term "daughter."

An Exodus of Sparks, section i. This poem is informed, in part, by Alex Wellerstein's article, "The First Light of Trinity," published in the *New Yorker* on July 16, 2015.

ACKNOWLEDGMENTS

If not for the care and guidance of many people and several institutions, this collection would not be in your hands. I wish to express my deepest gratitude to the staff at the RCAH Center for Poetry for understanding the necessity of poetry and community, to the team at Michigan State University Press for treating my work with such great care, and to the poet Roque Raquel Salas Rivera for validating it with their insight and understanding. Thank you to my support system: my daughter Tennyson, who revised my life into a thing of meaning and wonder; Jeff, who I love without measure; my siblings, who share my history and always keep me in their line of vision; and to Myo, who encouraged me through many paradigm shifts. Thank you to my earliest readers: Rooja Mohassessy, Allison Moore, James Ryder, Andrea Michalowsky, Megan Welch, and Joshua Boettiger; and the wonderful staff and faculty at Pacific University's MFA program, especially Kwame Dawes, Chris Abani, Joseph Millar, Dorianne Laux, and Jennifer Scanlon. Thank you to a number of people out in the world who might not suspect how much their actions have sustained me while writing, among them Lisa Jordan, Jerry Annen, and Jonathan Meiburg. I also wish to express gratitude to the editors and readers who supported this work as it appeared in the following journals:

Cathexis Northwest: "Cuckoldry"
December: "Revelations" and "A Life / Mislaid"
EcoTheo Review: "Daughter of Downwinders: II"
High Desert Journal: "Southeast of the Nevada Proving Ground"
Ilanot Review: "Forensic Ornithology"
Nine Mile Magazine: "Mogollon Rim," "The Appropriation of the Body of Moses," "The Assumption of the Body of Moses," and "Your Spirit Might Rise Up and Go Before You"
O:JA&L: "Exegesis" and "Here I Take"
Passengers: "Without Any Warning"
Plainsongs: "Stigmata"
Poetry South: "The 13th Article of Faith"
Rappahannock Review: "Hospitality"
Rust + Moth: "The Original Hyperlink Was the Word"
San Pedro River Review: "Depth of Field" and "Unsighted"
SWWIM: "Entropy Grips the Garden"
Tar River Poetry: "The Eros of Small Details"

The Account: "Bless the Damage"
The Journal: "An Exodus of Sparks: I"
The Maine Review: "Unreadable"
The Penn Review: "Let a Double Portion of Your Spirit Be Upon Me"
The Westchester Review: "The Cold that Settles Lifts" and "The Vessel and the Emanation"
The Worchester Review: "Slip"
Whale Road Review: "Ghost Ship on the Desert Floor"

SERIES ACKNOWLEDGMENTS

We at Wheelbarrow Books have many people to thank without whom *An Exodus of Sparks* would never be in your hands. We begin by thanking all those writers who submitted manuscripts to the fourteenth Wheelbarrow Books Prize for Poetry. We want to single out the finalists, Mary Ardery, Jennifer Bullis, Roxanne Cardona, Sandra Fees, Vivian Kao, K. T. Landon, and Pervin Saket, whose manuscripts moved and delighted us and which we passed onto the competition judge, Raquel Salas Rivera, for their final selection. Our thanks to Amaya Aten, Lillian Caister, Jenny Crakes, Allyson Davidson, Stephanie Glazer, Analise Krawczuk, and Jane Vincent Taylor for their careful reading of manuscripts and insightful commentary on their selections, and especially to Laurie Hollinger, acting director at the RCAH Center for Poetry, who also read the manuscripts and provided the logistical aid and financial wizardry for this project.

We go on to thank Elizabeth Demers, director of the Michigan State University Press, and the entire staff at the press who support the efforts of poets to continue reaching an eager audience and who produce these beautiful books to ferry their words out into the world. We cannot thank all of you enough for having the faith in us and the love of literature to collaborate on this project.

Thanks to our current Editorial Board, Sarah Bagby, Gabrielle Calvocoressi, Leila Chatti, Carol V. Davis, Mark Doty, George Ellenbogen, Carolyn Forche, Tyehimba Jess, George Ella Lyon, Thomas Lynch, Naomi Shihab Nye, and Raquel Salas Rivera for believing Wheelbarrow Books is a worthy undertaking and lending their support and their time to our success.

Finally, to our patrons: without your belief in the Wheelbarrow Books Poetry Series and your generous financial backing, we would still be sitting around the conference table adding up our loose change. You are making it possible for poets, when publishing a first volume of poetry is becoming harder and harder these days with so many presses discontinuing the publishing of poetry, to find an outlet for their work. Also, you are supporting the efforts of established poets to continue to reach a large and grateful audience. We name you here with great admiration and appreciation:

Beth Alexander	Fred Kraft
Gayle Davis	Jean Kreuger
Mary Hayden	Brian Teppen

Patricia and Robert Miller

There are many others whose smaller contributions we value whether those contributions come in terms of dollars, support for our programming, or promoting the books we have published and the writers we treasure. A special shout-out to Scott Harris, proprietor of Everybody Reads bookstore in Lansing, Michigan, for his continued support of Wheelbarrow Books through promotion and sales. Thank you, one and all.

WHEELBARROW BOOKS

Anita Skeen, *Series Editor*

Wheelbarrow Books, established in 2016, is an imprint of the RCAH Center for Poetry at Michigan State University, published and distributed by MSU Press. The biannual Wheelbarrow Books Poetry Prize is awarded every year to one emerging poet who has not yet published a first book and to one established poet.

SERIES EDITOR: Anita Skeen, professor in the Residential College in the Arts and Humanities (RCAH) at Michigan State University, founder and past director of the RCAH Center for Poetry, director of the Creative Arts Festival at Ghost Ranch, and director of the Fall Writing Festival.

The RCAH Center for Poetry opened in the fall of 2007 to encourage the reading, writing, and discussion of poetry and to create an awareness of the place and power of poetry in our everyday lives. We think about this in a number of ways, including through readings, performances, community outreach, and workshops. We believe that poetry is and should be fun, accessible, and meaningful. We are building a poetry community in the Greater Lansing area and beyond. Our undertaking of the Wheelbarrow Books Poetry Series is one of the gestures we make to aid in connecting good writers and eager readers beyond our regional boundaries. Information about the RCAH Center for Poetry at MSU can be found at http://poetry.rcah.msu.edu and also at https://centerforpoetry.wordpress.com and on Facebook and Twitter (@CenterForPoetry).

The mission of the Residential College in the Arts and Humanities at Michigan State University is to weave together the passion, imagination, humor, and candor of the arts and humanities to promote individual well-being and the common good. Students, faculty, and community partners in the arts and humanities have the power to focus critical attention on the public issues we face and the opportunities we have to resolve them. The arts and humanities not only give us the pleasure of living in the moment but also the wisdom to make sound judgments and good choices.

The mission, then, is to see things as they are, to hear things as others may, to tell these stories as they should be told, and to contribute to the making of a better world. The Residential College in the Arts and Humanities is built on four cornerstones: world history, art and culture, ethics, and engaged learning. Together they define an open-minded public space within which students, faculty, staff, and community partners can explore today's common problems and create shared moral visions of the future. Discover more about the Residential College in the Arts and Humanities at Michigan State at http://rcah.msu.edu.